目 次

1、手で回転させる事の出来るコップ------------------------------------ 3

　使用方法及び概要

　　The glass which I can turn by hand------------------------------ 7

　　　Usage and summary

2、回転コップ＆回転クルリコップの色々な使用方法--------------------11

　⑴　見合いの盛上り--11

　⑵　ゲームの楽しさ--12

　⑶　懇親会の盛上り--13

　⑷　ギャンブル予想--14

　⑸　占い--15

　⑹　会話の盛上り--16

　⑺　くじ予想--17

　⑻　順番を決める--18

　⑼　じゃん拳大会--19

Various directions for a rotation glass

　Top of the marriage meeting-------------------------------------21

　Pleasure of a game---22

　Climax of a social gathering-----------------------------------23

　Gamble expectation---24

　Fortune-telling--25

　Climax of conversation---26

　Lot anticipatio--27

Determination of turn---28

　　'Let's toss(up)for it' great meeting------------------------------------29

3、公報解説　手で回転させる事が出来るコップ------------------------------30

　　⑴　要約・課題--30

　　⑵　解決手段--30

　　⑶　実用新案登録請求の範囲--30

　　⑷　考案の詳細な説明--31

　　⑸　考案概要・技術分野--31

　　⑹　背景技術--31

　　⑺　考案が解決しょうとする課題--31

　　⑻　課題を解決するための手段--32

　　⑼　考案の効果--32

　　⑽　図面の簡単な説明--32

　　⑾　符号の説明--32

　　⑿　手続補正書--35

　　JPO and INPIT are not responsible for any ----------------------------39

　　damages caused by the use of this translation.

１、手で回転させる事の出来るコップ

使用方法及び概要

○　現在市販されているコップ類の中に、コップ自身が回転するものは見当たらない。

一般的にコップ自身は動かずテーブルの上などに安定して置く事を目的として作られているのが常識である。

そのコップに回転する機能を持たせ、手で回すことが出来るようにしたものであり、カラのコップや飲み物の入ったコップを回転させ、回るコップとして使用する事が出来、また、回転させなければ普通のコップとしても使用する事が出来る。

コップの底の中心(外側)に小さな突起を設け、その突起を軸にコップを手で回してやればコップは自重と底の中心の軸と外周部分とでバランス良く安定した回転をする。

○　その回転する特徴を生かしコップの側面に色々な要素を取り入れて付加価値のあるコップとする。

コップの側面にデザインやキャラクター・模様などを描き、回転させる事によって、そのデザインやキャラクター・模様などに動きを与えると共に、回転するコップのデザインやキャラクター・

模様などの凹凸に、光が屈折や反射する事で、よりコップに動きを感じさせる事が出来る。

又、デザインやキャラクター・模様などと合わせてコップの側面下部近くに記号やマーク・文字等を横に，等間隔に数個描き回転させて正面で止まった位置のコ

ップの記号やマーク・文字などを見て楽しむゲームや占いなども行う事ができる。

【図1】考案の斜視図

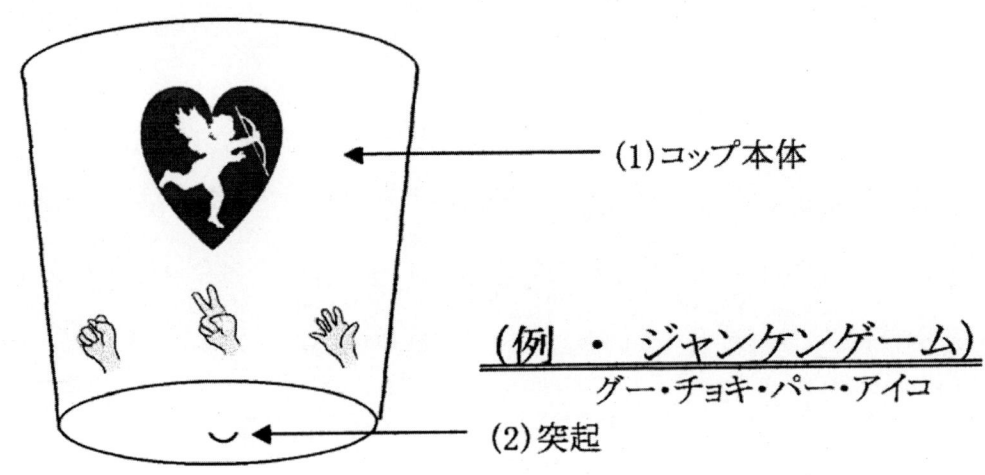

【図2】考案の正面図、背面、左右側面図

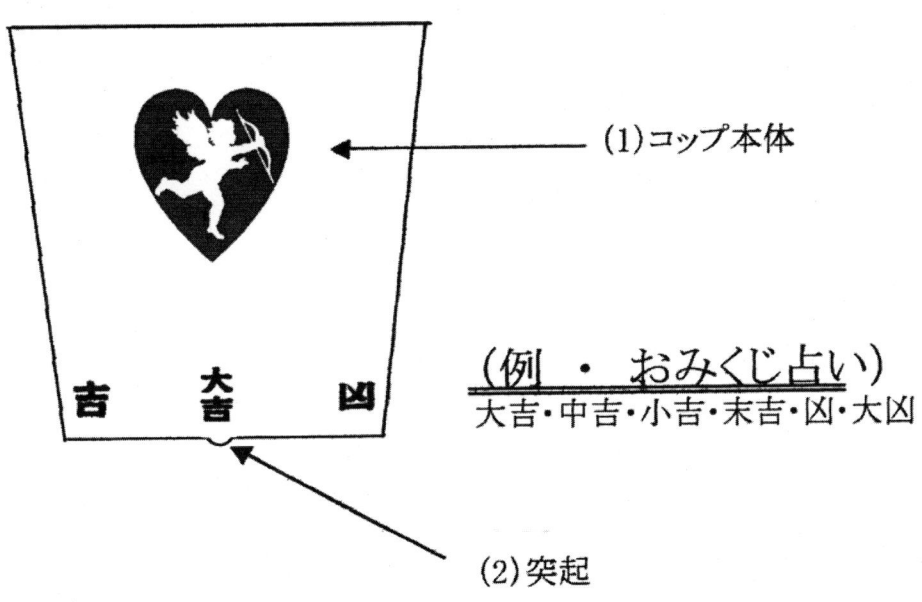

【図3】考案の底面図

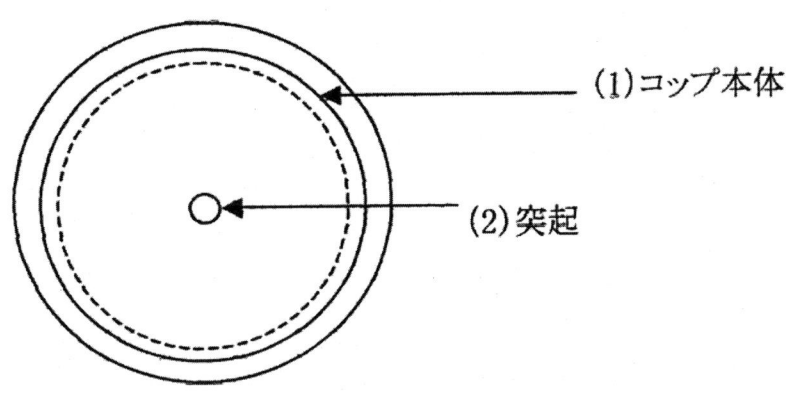

〇回転するコップは大人から子どもまで興味をもって楽しんで使うことが出来るもので、現在市販されている色々なデザインや形のコップは飲み物を入れて使用する事のみを目的として作られているが、もしそれらのコップが回転すればそれだけで楽しいものになる。

〇食堂やレストラン、ホテルや旅館のコップ、喫茶店、スナック、屋台、などのたくさんのコップが回転し、なにより我が家でジュースを飲むコップや、晩酌で飲むビールのコップが回れば、楽しいものである、合わせてゲームや占いが出来るとなればなおさらである。

〇国内でも国外でも話題となり早い時期に現在市販されて流通しているたくさんのコップに取って代わる事が出来るものであり、経済的に効果は非常に大きく期待出来る物である。

The glass which I can turn by hand

Usage and summary

There is nothing that rotates with a commercial glass.

Generally, the glass is made so that it may be stabilized.

The glass of Calah and the glass containing a drink are rotated and it can be used as a usual glass.

projection is formed in the center of the bottom of a glass, and the projection becomes an axis and rotates.

It turns by hand and makes it rotate.

A game is possible in the lateral pattern of a turning glass.

A game is made in the pattern of the side of the rotating glass.

The pattern and character of the side of the rotating glass give a motion.

Touch that the glass is running by refraction of light, and reflection.

When a rotation glass stops, it divines in the pattern of the side, and a character and can enjoy a game.

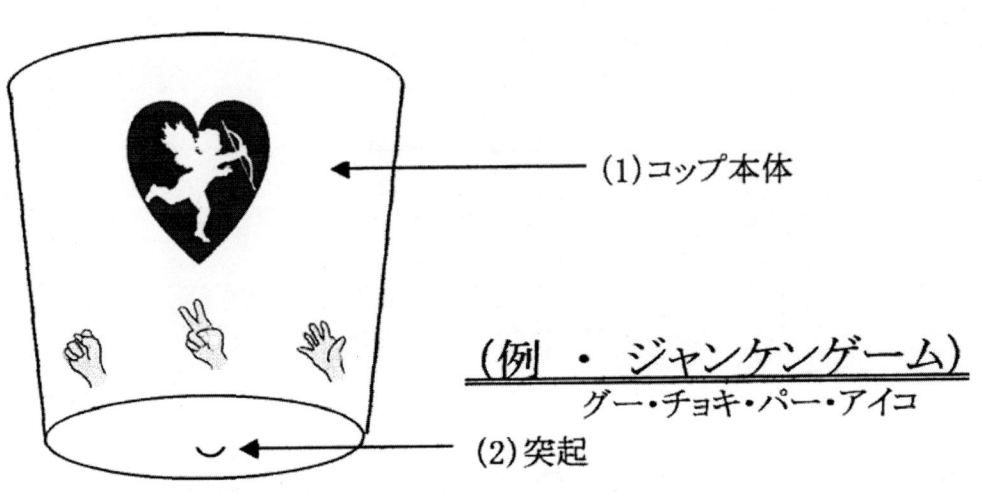

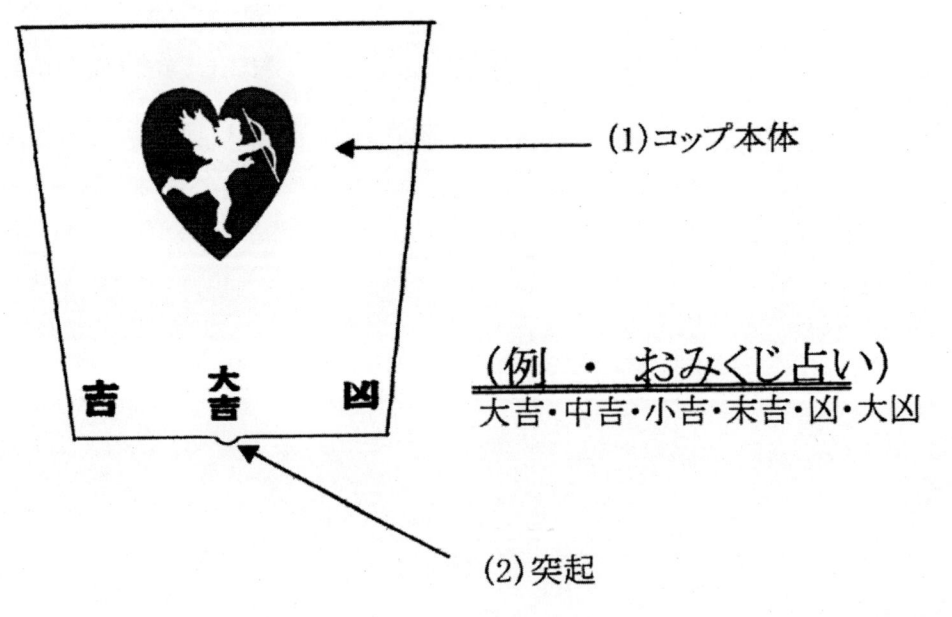

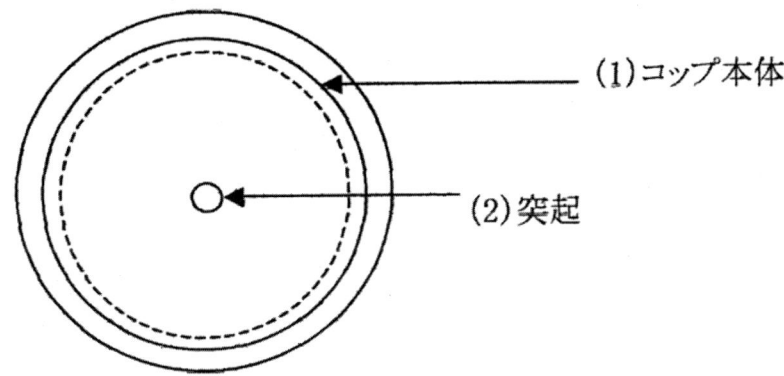

The rotation glass can have and enjoy interest from an adult to a child.

It is prosperity in business, enjoying a game in a rotation glass in a restaurant, a snack, and a tavern.

Also overseas [domestic], this rotation glass becomes the center of attention, and can expect an economical effect.

２、回転コップ＆回転クルリコップの色々な使用方法

(1) 見合いの盛上り

恋人同士の回転クルリコップのゲームが楽しい。

(2) ゲームの楽しさ

　スタンドバーのカウンターで一人、回転コップでゲームをしながらお酒を飲む楽しさ。

(3) 懇親会の盛上り

　居酒屋で回転コップで、じゃん拳をする盛上り。

⑷　ギャンブル予想

　回転コップで水を飲みながらギャンブル予想の出目を絞る。

(5) 占い

　回転クルリコップに聖水を入れて、人生の凶・吉を占う。

(6) 会話の盛上り

スナックで盛り上がる回転コップのゲーム。

⑺　くじ予想

　宝くじロトの予想、回転クルリコップで楽しさ倍増。

⑻　順番を決める

　カラオケバーで歌う順番を回転コップで決める。

⑼　じゃん拳大会

　回転コップのじゃん拳大会で、強い人、弱い人の差がない面白い展開。

Various directions for a rotation glass

(1)

Top of the marriage meeting

The game of lovers' rotation glass is pleasant.

(2)

Pleasure of a game

Pleasure which drinks alcohol while acting as one person at the counter of a bar with only a counter and playing a game in a rotation glass.

(3)

Climax of a social gathering

Climax which carries out 'Let's toss(up)for it' in a rotation glass in a tavern

(4)

Gamble expectation

The projecting eyes of gamble anticipation are extracted in a rotation glass.

(5)

Fortune-telling

Holy water is put into rotation Grass and the ill luck and 吉 of life are divined.

(6)

Climax of conversation

The game of the rotation glass which rises for a snack

(7)

Lot anticipatio

Pleasure doubles with the expectation of the public lottery lot, rotary Kuril glass

(8)

Determination of turn

decide a turn to sing in a karaoke bar with a rotary glass.

(9)

'Let's toss(up)for it' great meeting

Interesting deployment which does not have a difference of a strong person and a weak person in the 'Let's toss(up)for it great meeting of a rotation glass.

公報解説　手で回転させる事の出来るコップ

手で回転させる事の出来るコップ・

考案の名称；実用新案登録第３１７２５７５号

実用新案権者／考案者；湯谷　久雄

(1)【要約】【課題】

コップの底の外側の面の中心に突起を設け、その突起を軸にして、視覚的楽しみのためコップを手で回して回転させることができるコップを提供する。

(2)【解　決手段】

コップの底の外側の面の中心につけた突起を軸に回転する様にコップを形成する。前記突起は丸形や三角、又花形などでありその突起の中心がコップの　底の外周より少し出す。具体的には、コップの大きさや底の直径によって異なるが、０．１～１．０mmの範囲で、それぞれのコップの大きさにおいて安定した　回転を得ることが出来る高さの突起を持っていることを特徴として該コップを形成する。

【選択図】図１

(3)【実用新案登録請求の範囲】

【請求項１】

グラスの底の外側の中心についた突起を軸に回転するグラス（コップ、タンブラー）

【請求項２】

［請求項１］の突起とは丸型や三角、又デザイン（花形など）でその中心がグラス

の底の外周より少し出ている突起。

【請求項3】

［請求項1］の突起の高さは、グラスの大きさや底の直径によって異なるが、０．１～１．０mmの範囲でそれぞれの大きさにおいて安定した回転を得られることが出来る。

【請求項4】

［請求項1］のグラス（コップ、タンブラー）の材質は、ガラス、金属、プラスチックなどでつくられたもの。

(4)【考案の詳細な説明】

(5)【考案概要】【技術分野】

【０００１】

この考案はグラス（コップ・タンブラー）の底の中心に突起を付けた回転グラス（コップ・タンブラー）に関するものである。

(6)【背景技術】

【０００２】

従来は平らな所で飲み物を入れて飲んだり、整理・整頓して置くことを目的としたグラス（コップ・タンブラー）であった。

(7)【考案が解決しようとする課題】

【０００３】

飲み物を飲むためにボトルなどからグラス（コップ・タンブラー）に小分けして出して飲んだり、それを静止させて置く事だけを目的とするのではなく、動きを与え

て目でも楽しむ事が出来るようにする。

(8)【課題を解決するための手段】

【０００４】

グラス（コップ・タンブラー）の底の外側の面の中心に突起を設け、その突起を軸にし手でグラス（コップ・タンブラー）を回転させる。

(9)【考案の効果】

【０００５】

グラス（コップ・タンブラー）が回転するので飲み物を入れた時だけでなく、グラス（コップ・タンブラー）の外周に絵や文字、キャラクター等を描き、そのグラス（コップ・タンブラー）を回転させ絵や文字、キャラクターに動きを与えて楽しむことができる。

又、グラス等の外周に大吉、中吉、小吉、吉、末吉などを描き回転を与えて正面で止まった所を見て占うおみくじ占いや、グー、チョキ、パー、あいこ、などを描き、回転させ止った位置を見て勝ち負けを決めるジャンケンゲームなど、いろいろな占いやゲームを楽しむことが出来る。

(10)【図面の簡単な説明】

【０００６】

【図１】考案の斜視図である。

【図２】考案の正面、背面図、左右側面図である。

【図３】考案の底面図である。

(11)【符号の説明】

【０００７】

1．グラス本体

2．突起

考案の斜視図である。

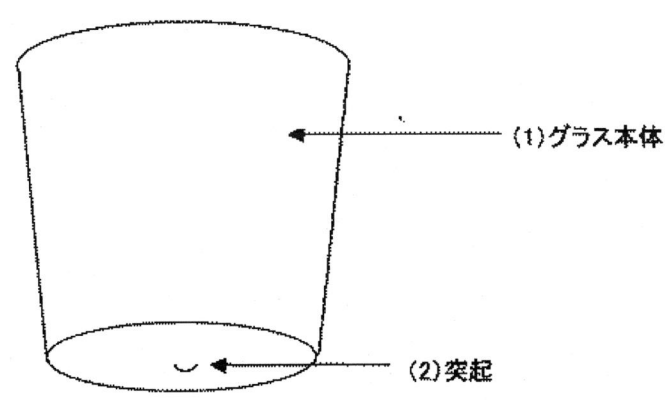

考案の正面、背面図、左右側面図である。

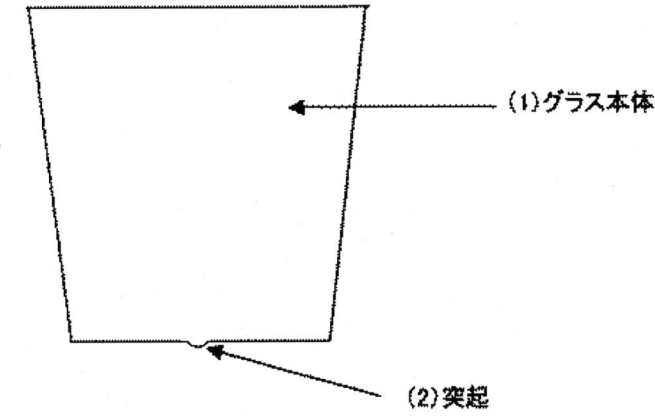

考案の底面図である。

(1)グラス

(2)突起

⑿【手続補正書】

【提出日】平成23年10月5日（2011．10．5）

【手続補正1】

【補正対象書類名】実用新案登録請求の範囲

【補正対象項目名】全文

【補正方法】変更

【補正の内容】

【実用新案登録請求の範囲】

【請求項1】

コップの底の外側の面の中心につけた突起を軸に回転するコップ。

【請求項2】

前記突起は丸形や三角、又花形などでありその突起の中心がコップの底の外周より少し出ていることを特徴とする請求項1に記載のコップ。

【請求項3】

前記突起の高さは、コップの大きさや底の直径によって異なるが、0．1～1．0mmの範囲で、それぞれのコップの大きさにおいて安定した回転を得ることが出来る高さの突起を持っていることを特徴とした請求項1に記載のコップ。

【請求項4】

前記のコップの材質は、ガラス、金属、プラスチック等であることを特徴とした請求項1に記載のコップ。

【手続補正2】

【補正対象書類名】明細書

【補正対象項目名】全文

【補正方法】変更

【補正の内容】

【考案の詳細な説明】

【考案概要】

【技術分野】

【０００１】

この考案はコップの底の外側の面の中心に突起をつけた手で回転させる事の出来るコップに関するものである。

【背景技術】

【０００２】

従来のものは平らな所で飲み物を入れて飲んだり、整理・整頓して置くことを目的としたコップであった。

【考案が解決しようとする課題】

【０００３】

飲み物を飲むときに保存容器やボトルなどからコップに注いで飲んだり、そのまま静止状態にして置く事だけを目的とするのではなく、手でコップにまわる力を与えてコップを回転させコップの動きを目で見て楽しむ事が出来るようにする。

【課題を解決するための手段】

【０００４】

コップの底の外側の面の中心に突起を設け、その突起を軸にしてコップを手で回して回転させる。

【考案の効果】

【０００５】

コップが回転するので飲み物を入れ回転させるだけでなく、コップの側面に絵や文字、キャラクター等を描き、そのコップを回転させ絵や文字、キャラクターに動きを与えてそれらを見て楽しむことができる。

又コップの側面に大吉・中吉・小吉・吉・末吉などを描き回転を与えて正面で止まった所を見て占うおみくじ占いや、グー・チョキ・パー・アイコ等を描いて回転させ止った位置を見て勝ち負けを決めるジャンケンゲームなど、いろいろな占いやゲームを楽しむことが出来る。

【図面の簡単な説明】

【０００６】

【図１】考案の斜視図である。

【図２】考案の正面、背面、左右側面図である。

【図３】考案の底面図である。

【符号の説明】

【０００７】

（１）　コップ本体

（２）　突起

【手続補正３】

【補正対象書類名】図面

【補正対象項目名】全図

【補正方法】変更

【補正の内容】

【図１】

考案の斜視図である。

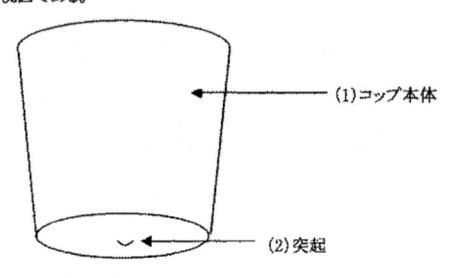

(1)コップ本体
(2)突起

考案の正面、背面、左右側面図である。

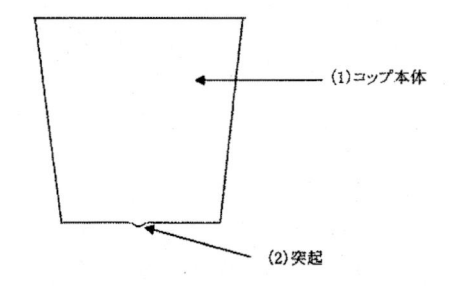

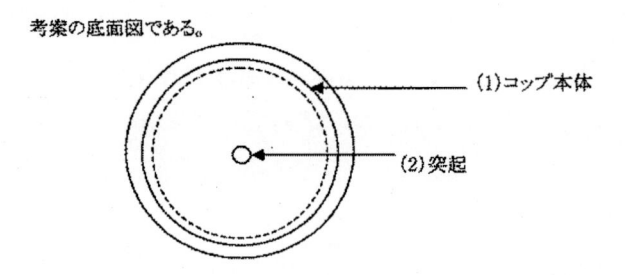

(1)コップ本体
(2)突起

考案の底面図である。

(1)コップ本体
(2)突起

JPO and INPIT are not responsible for any damages caused by the use of this translation.

1. This document has been translated by computer. So the translation may not reflect the original precisely.

2. **** shows the word which can not be translated.

3. In the drawings, any words are not translated.

DETAILED DESCRIPTION

[Detailed explanation of the device]

[Device outline]

[Field of the Invention]

[0001]

This device is related with the rotation glass (glass tumbler) which attached the projection to the center of the bottom of a glass (glass tumbler).

[Background of the Invention]

[0002]

It was a glass (glass tumbler) aiming at putting in and drinking, or carrying out house keeping of the drink and placing it conventionally, in an even place.

[Problem(s) to be Solved by the Device]

[0003]

It does not aim only at subdividing into a glass (glass tumbler), taking out from a bottle etc., drinking, or making it stand it still and placing in order to drink a drink, but he gives a motion, and it enables it to enjoy itself also by the eye.

[Means for solving problem]

[0004]

A projection is provided at the center of the surface of the outside of the bottom of a glass (glass tumbler), and a glass (glass tumbler) is rotated by hand centering on the projection.

[Effect of the Device]

[0005]

A picture, a character, a character, etc. are drawn on the periphery of since the glass (glass tumbler) rotated, not only when a drink is put in, but a glass (glass tumbler), the glass (glass tumbler) can be rotated, and a motion can be given and enjoyed in a picture, a character, and a character.

Sacred-oracle fortune-telling who looks at and divines the place which drew Daikichi, average luck, moderate luck, **, Sueyoshi, etc. on the periphery of a glass etc., gave rotation, and stopped at the transverse plane, Various fortune-tellings and games, such as good one, CHOKI, a par, and a JANKEN game that looks at the position which suited, drew ** etc., made it rotate and stopped, and determines victory and defeat, can be enjoyed.

[Brief Description of the Drawings]

[0006]

  [Drawing 1]It is a perspective view of a device.

[Drawing 2]They are a transverse plane of a device, a rear elevation, and a left-and-right-laterals figure.

[Drawing 3]It is a bottom view of a device.

[Explanations of letters or numerals]

[0007]

1. Main part of glass

2. Projection

CLAIMS

[Claims]

[Claim 1]

A glass which rotates centering on a projection attached to the center of the outside of a bottom of a glass (a glass, tumbler)

[Claim 2]

A projection out of which the center has come for a while from a periphery of a bottom of a glass by round shape, triangle, and designs (star etc.) with a projection of [Claim 1].

[Claim 3]

Although height of a projection of [Claim 1] changes with a size of a glass, or diameters of a bottom, it can obtain rotation stable in each size in 0.1-1.0 mm.

[Claim 4]

That with which construction material of a glass (a glass, tumbler) of [Claim 1] was built with glass, metal, a plastic, etc.

WRITTEN AMENDMENT

[Written Amendment]

[Filing date]Heisei 23(2011) October 5 (2011.10.5)

[Amendment 1]

[Document to be Amended]Claims

[Item(s) to be Amended]Whole sentence

[Method of Amendment]Change

[The contents of correction]

[Claims]

[Claim 1]

A glass which rotates centering on a projection attached to the center of a surface of the outside of a bottom of a glass.

[Claim 2]

The glass according to claim 1 which the aforementioned projections are a round shape, a triangle, a star, etc., and is characterized by the center of the projection having come out for a while from a periphery of a bottom of a glass.

[Claim 3]

The glass according to claim 1 although it changes [height of the aforementioned projection] with a size of a glass, or diameters of a bottom, wherein it has the projection of height which can obtain rotation which a range of is 0.1-1.0 mm, and was stabilized in a size of each glass.

[Claim 4]

The glass according to claim 1, wherein construction material of the aforementioned glass is glass, metal, a plastic, etc.

[Amendment 2]

[Document to be Amended]Description

[Item(s) to be Amended]Whole sentence

[Method of Amendment]Change

[The contents of correction]

[Detailed explanation of the device]

[Device outline]

[Field of the Invention]

[0001]

This device is related with the glass which can be rotated by the hand which attached the projection to the center of the surface of the outside of the bottom of a glass.

[Background of the Invention]

[0002]

The conventional thing was a glass aiming at putting in and drinking, or carrying out house keeping of the drink and placing it in an even place.

[Problem(s) to be Solved by the Device]

[0003]

When drinking a drink, it does not aim only at flowing into a glass from a preservation container, a bottle, etc., drinking, or using a state of rest as it is, and placing, but the power which turns to a glass by hand is given, and a glass is rotated, and a motion of a glass is seen by the eye and it enables it to enjoy it.

[Means for solving problem]

[0004]

A projection is provided at the center of the surface of the outside of the bottom of a glass, and a glass is turned by hand and it is made to rotate centering on the projection.

[Effect of the Device]

[0005]

Since a glass rotates, it draws a picture, a character, a character, etc. on the side surface of a glass, and the glass can be rotated, and it can give a motion to a picture, a character, and a character, and it puts in a drink and not only can make it rotate, but can see and enjoy them.

Various fortune-tellings and games, such as sacred-oracle fortune-telling who looks at and divines the place which drew Daikichi, Nakayoshi, moderate luck, **, Sueyoshi, etc. on the side surface of a glass, gave rotation, and stopped at the transverse plane, and a JANKEN game which looks at the position which drew and rotated good CHOKI Per Aikoh etc. and stopped, and determines victory and defeat, can be enjoyed.

[Brief Description of the Drawings]

[0006]

[Drawing 1]It is a perspective view of a device.

[Drawing 2]They are a transverse plane of a device, a back face, and a left-and-right-laterals figure.

[Drawing 3]It is a bottom view of a device.

[Explanations of letters or numerals]

[0007]

(1) The main part of a glass

(2) Projection

[Amendment 3]

[Document to be Amended]DRAWINGS

[Item(s) to be Amended]Complete diagram

[Method of Amendment]Change

[The contents of correction]

[Drawing 1]

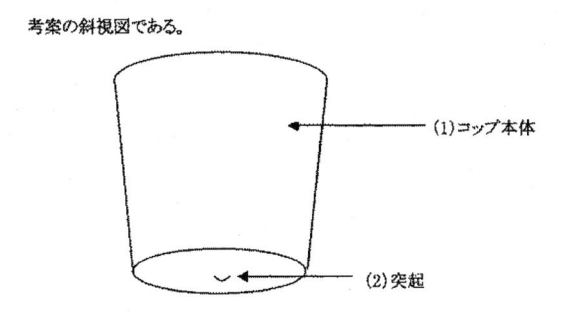

[Drawing 2]

考案の正面、背面、左右側面図である。

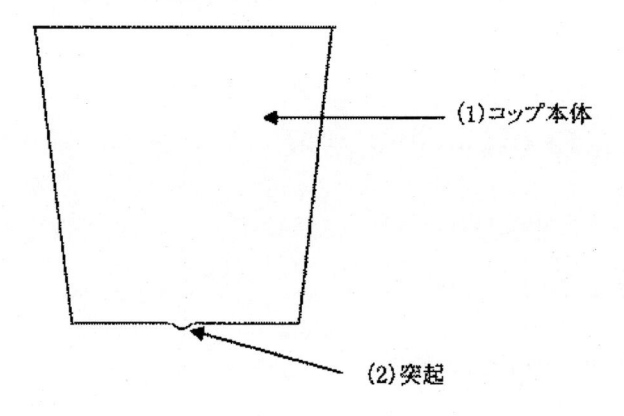

(1)コップ本体

(2)突起

[Drawing 3]

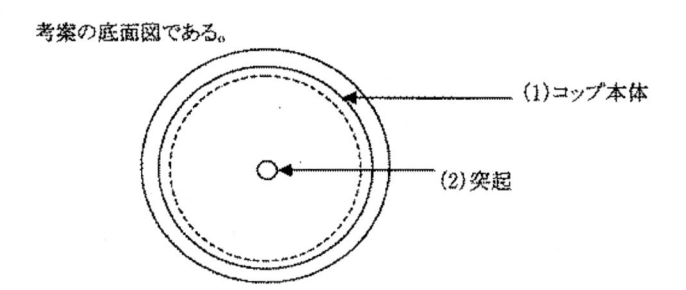

考案の底面図である。

(1)コップ本体

(2)突起

回転クルリ・コップの使用方法

定価（本体1,000円＋税）

―――――――――――――――――――――――――――――

２０１２年（平成２４年）１１月３０日発行

発行所　発明開発連合会®

東京都渋谷区渋谷 2-2-13

電話 03-3498-0751㈹

発行人　ましば寿一

No. UT-026

Printed in Japan

著者　湯谷久雄 ©

―――――――――――――――――――――――――――――

本書の一部または全部を無断で複写、複製、転載、データーファイル化することを禁じています。

It forbids a copy, a duplicate, reproduction, and forming a data file for some or all of this book without notice.